THE HORSE GIRL'S
FUN FACT BOOK

Everything Kids Should
Know About Horses

LEMON COOKS

lemon cooks

Once upon a time...
...in a quaint little town, there was a small but loving family known as the Lemons. The Lemon family, consisting of Anna, a talented illustrator, her husband Mark, a skilled writer, and their two imaginative children, Lily and Max, shared a deep passion for creativity and learning.

Their story began one sunny afternoon when Lily and Max were busy coloring at the kitchen table. Mark was scribbling away at a story, and Anna was sketching some cheerful characters. As they worked, an idea sparked in Anna's mind. "What if we combined our talents to create something special?" she suggested excitedly. The family agreed, and the Lemon Cooks brand was born.

Their first project was a coloring book, filled with Anna's delightful illustrations and sprinkled with Mark's whimsical words. They decided to publish it on Amazon KDP, a platform they learned could reach families across the globe. To their delight, the book was a hit, especially with kids who loved the blend of storytelling and art.

Encouraged by their success, the Lemons expanded their offerings. They created activity books that taught children about nature, science, and art. They also developed journals and planners, believing in the power of writing to organize and improve one's life.

The Lemon Cooks brand stood out because it wasn't just about selling books; it was about sharing a piece of their family's heart and creativity with the world. Each book was crafted with care, love, and the intention to bring joy and learning into homes.

As the brand grew, so did its impact. Families from different parts of the world sent letters expressing gratitude. Children shared drawings inspired by the books, and parents thanked the Lemons for providing tools that brought their families closer together.

The Lemon Cooks brand remained true to its roots as a small family brand.

Anna, Mark, Lily, and Max continued to collaborate, always finding new ways to inspire and uplift others. They showed that with creativity, love, and a bit of lemony zest, even a small family brand could make a big difference in the world. And so, the Lemon Cooks continued to spread happiness, one book at a time.

THIS BOOK BELONGS TO:

TABLE OF CONTENTS:

CHAPTER 1

MEET THE HORSES

Horses come in many different types, each with its own unique features and markings. Let's explore some fascinating facts about horse breeds, fur, and markings that make them special and beautiful!

1. Palominos have golden fur that shines like the sun.

2. Appaloosas have spots all over their bodies, like a leopard.

3. Dapple Grays have coats covered in little circles, like polka dots.

4. Paints have big patches of different colors on their fur.

5. Pintos have a mix of white and another color, like a fancy costume.

6.
Bay horses have a dark brown coat with black points on their legs, ears, and mane.

7.

Tobiano horses have big, splashy colored patches on their bodies.

8.

Roan horses have sprinkles of color all over their fur.

9.

Chestnut horses have a warm reddish-brown coat.

10.

Friesian horses are big and beautiful with shiny black fur and long, flowing manes.

TEST YOUR KNOWLEDGE!

Did you really absorb the new facts you have read about horses in this chapter?
Try answering the questions below:

What do you call horses with big patches of different colors on their fur?

A Appaloosas   **B** Paints   **C** Palominos

What do you call horses with shiny black fur and long, flowing manes?

A Friesian   **B** Persian   **C** Freesian

CHAPTER 2

HORSE TALK

Horse communication involves a variety of sounds, such as neighs and whinnies, as well as body language expressed through their ears, tails, and eyes. Let's explore some simple and fascinating facts about how horses talk and express themselves!

1.

Horses talk to each other with sounds like neighs and whinnies, just like we talk with words!

2.

When a horse's ears are forward, they're happy and curious, but if they're pinned back, they might be mad or scared.

3.

If a horse wags its tail, it might mean they're feeling playful or excited.

4.

Horses can use their big, round eyes to show if they're scared or surprised.

5.

When a horse stomps its hooves, it could mean they're feeling impatient or annoyed.

6.

Sometimes horses snort loudly to show they're feeling confident or happy.

14

7.

If a horse is flicking its ears back and forth, they might be listening carefully to something.

8.

Horses can make soft nickering sounds to greet their friends or ask for food.

9.

When a horse arches its neck and pricks its ears, it might mean they're feeling proud or showing off.

10.

Horses might gently nuzzle each other to show they care and want to be friends!

TEST YOUR KNOWLEDGE!

Did you really absorb the new facts you have read about horses in this chapter?
Try answering the questions below:

A loud snort from a horse may mean...

A Confidence   **B** Gloominess   **C** Shyness

When a horse is feeling impatient or annoyed...

A They wag their tail.   **B** They stomp their hooves.   **C** They wiggle their ears.

CHAPTER 3
FOALS & FAMILIES

Let's learn about some fun facts about horse families and how foals grow, play, and learn together. From adorable foal antics to the heartwarming bonds within horse herds, there's so much to discover about these fascinating creatures!

1.

While human babies take 9 months to be born, horse foals take 11 months.

2.

Horse foals love to play games like tag and chase with their brothers and sisters.

3.

Foals have strong legs to run and jump, and they can walk and trot only a few hours after birth.

4.

Horses live in families called herds, where they take care of each other.

5.

Baby horses stick close to their moms for safety and also to drink milk.

6.
Mother horses usually give birth very quickly, taking only around 15 minutes, and usually happening at night!

7.
Families of horses like to groom each other by gently scratching with their teeth.

8.
Foals make cute little whinny sounds to call for their moms when they're scared.

9.
The lead stallion, a male horse, usually guards the mother horse and her foal.

10.
Mother horses educate by nipping her baby's rear, squealing, or shoving with her head.

TEST YOUR KNOWLEDGE!

Did you really absorb the new facts you have
read about horses in this chapter?
Try answering the questions below:

Mother horses give birth quickly, around...

A 15 minutes   **B** 30 minutes   **C** 90 minutes

A male horse is called...

A Pony   **B** Mare   **C** Stallion

CHAPTER 4

FEEDING THE STEED

Let's explore the relationship between what horses eat and their health. From nutritious snacks to harmful foods, understanding what fuels these magnificent animals can keep them happy and healthy.

1.

Carrots are like crunchy snacks for horses, packed with vitamins that keep their eyes and skin healthy.

2.

Apples are not only delicious but also help keep a horse's teeth strong and their breath fresh.

3.

Oats are a favorite food of horses, providing them with energy to run and play all day long.

4.

Raisins are an enjoyable treat for horses, unlike pet dogs who will may experience poisoning if they eat raisins.

5.

Fresh grass is like a buffet for horses, full of nutrients that help them grow strong muscles and bones.

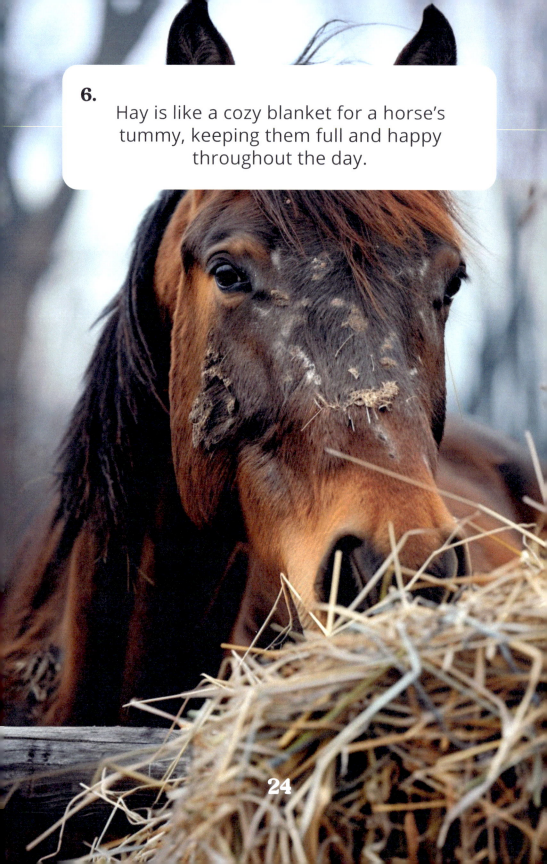

6.

Hay is like a cozy blanket for a horse's tummy, keeping them full and happy throughout the day.

7.

Horses shouldn't eat chocolate because it can make them sick— it's toxic to them.

8.

Onions can upset a horse's stomach and cause them to feel unwell.

9.

Some plants, like ragwort and foxglove, are poisonous to horses and can make them very sick if eaten.

10.

Sugary treats like cookies and cakes can upset a horse's stomach and lead to health problems.

TEST YOUR KNOWLEDGE!

Did you really absorb the new facts you have read about horses in this chapter?
Try answering the questions below:

This horse snack keeps their eyesight sharp.

A Carrots   **B** Onions   **C** Beans

Which of these plants is not dangerous for horses?

A Ragwort   **B** Foxglove   **C** Grass

CHAPTER 5

GALLOP GROUNDS

Let's read about what horses call home, both in the wild and in the shelters humans provide for them. From vast open plains to cozy barns, these habitats play a crucial role in ensuring their well-being.

1.
Wild horses roam across wide-open areas called grasslands, where they can find plenty of yummy grass to eat.

2.
Some wild horses live in places with lots of trees and bushes, called forests, where they can find shelter from the weather.

3.
Horses might also make their homes in rocky areas called mountains, where they can climb and explore.

4.
Wild horses are experts at finding water sources like rivers and ponds, which they need to drink to stay hydrated.

5.
The Namib horse is a special breed that lives in the harsh Namib Desert, where water and food are scarce.

6.
Barns are cozy shelters made by humans for horses, providing protection from the weather.

29

7.

Stables are smaller shelters where horses can rest and sleep comfortably at night.

8.

Paddocks are fenced areas where horses can move around freely and graze on grass.

9.

Pastures are large fields where horses can roam and play together in sunshine.

10.

Arenas are areas where horses and riders can practice riding and jumping over obstacles.

TEST YOUR KNOWLEDGE!

Did you really absorb the new facts you have read about horses in this chapter? Try answering the questions below:

These are large fields where horses can roam and play.

A Pasture   **B** Paddocks   **C** Courtyard

These are smaller than barns, where horses can rest and sleep.

A Stable   **B** Cage   **C** Coop

CHAPTER 6
FIT & FABULOUS

Let's delve into the world of horse health and fitness, exploring exercises to keep these magnificent animals strong and vibrant, as well as common diseases.

1.

Trotting is a type of horse exercise where they move at a steady, bouncy pace, helping to strengthen their leg muscles.

2.

Galloping is when horses run fast, stretching their muscles and building up their stamina.

3.

Lunging is like horse aerobics, where they move around in circles on a long rope to warm up and stretch their muscles.

4.

Jumping is a fun exercise where horses leap over obstacles, using their leg muscles to propel them into the air.

5.

Dressage is a fancy exercise where horses perform elegant movements like dancing, showing off their strength and agility.

6.
Colic is a tummy ache that horses can get if they eat too fast or something disagrees with them—walking them gently and calling a vet can help.

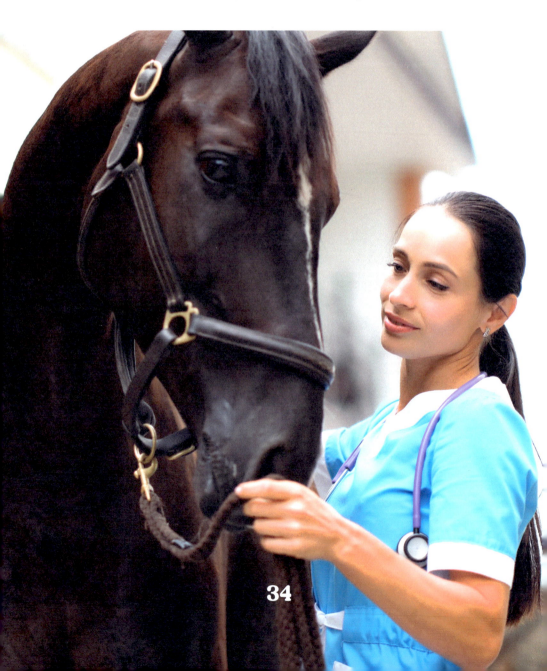

7.

Lameness is when a horse has trouble walking because of sore muscles or a hurt leg.

8.

Thrush is a yucky infection in a horse's hooves caused by bacteria.

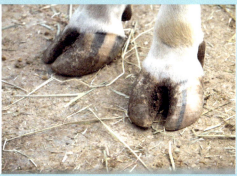

9.

Founder is a painful condition where a horse's hooves get sore and inflamed

10.

Colitis is a serious sickness that affects a horse's intestines, needing immediate veterinary help.

TEST YOUR KNOWLEDGE!

Did you really absorb the new facts you have read about horses in this chapter?
Try answering the questions below:

Horse movement described as a steady, bouncy pace.

A Bouncing   **B** Galloping   **C** Trotting

This is when a horse has trouble walking because of sore or hurt leg.

A Lethargy   **B** Lameness   **C** Colitis

CHAPTER 7

HOOVES ACROSS HISTORY

Let's journey through history and culture with horses, exploring their remarkable roles alongside humans. From ancient battles to modern-day festivals, horses have left hoofprints on our hearts and history books alike.

1.

War horses were brave companions to soldiers, carrying them into battle and charging fearlessly into the fray.

2.

Workhorses helped plow fields and pull heavy loads, making farming easier for humans.

3.

Riding horses carried people on long journeys, helping them travel across vast distances.

4.

Carriage horses pulled fancy carriages for rich people, parading them through the streets in style.

5.

In ancient art, horses are presented as animals with prestige and importance, often appearing in paintings with royalty.

6.

The Kentucky Derby is a famous horse race in the United States, where horses sprint around a track to win a big prize.

7.
The Calgary Stampede is a fun festival in Canada, featuring rodeo events like horse barrel racing.

8.
The Luminarias Festival in Spain celebrates horses with colorful parades and performances.

9.
The Naadam Festival includes horse racing as one of its traditional sports using Mongolian horses.

10.
The White Turf event in Switzerland is a unique horse race held on a frozen lake.

TEST YOUR KNOWLEDGE!

Did you really absorb the new facts you have read about horses in this chapter?
Try answering the questions below:

A carriage horse carries what?

A Fancy carriages

B Carts of cargo

C Carpentry materials

Which of these countries was not mentioned in the chapter to celebrate horses?

A Switzerland

B Spain

C Philippines

CHAPTER 8

LEGENDS OF LORE

Embark on a mythical adventure as we delve into the world of horse characters from ancient myths and legends. From flying steeds to magical creatures, these legendary equines are characters of grand design.

1.

Pegasus is a winged horse from Greek mythology, born from the blood of Medusa, and known for his ability to fly.

2.

Sleipnir is an eight-legged horse from Norse mythology, ridden by the god Odin, who could travel between worlds.

3.

The Kelpie is a shape-shifting water horse from Scottish folklore, often appearing to lure people into rivers or lakes.

4.

The Unicorn is a mythical horse with a magical horn on its forehead, believed to have healing powers.

5.

The Hippocampus is a sea horse from Greek mythology, with the upper body of a horse and the tail of a fish.

6.

Arion is a legendary horse from Greek mythology, known for his incredible speed and beauty.

7.

The Kinnara is a horse-like creature from Hindu and Buddhist mythology, known for its musical talents.

8.

The Chollima is a legendary horse from Korean folklore, capable of running long distances.

9.

The Centaur is a creature from Greek myths with the upper body of a human and the lower body of a horse.

10.

From legend, King Arthur had a mare called Llamrei and a stallion called Hengroen.

TEST YOUR KNOWLEDGE!

Did you really absorb the new facts you have read about horses in this chapter?
Try answering the questions below:

Who is the eight-legged horse from Norse mythology?

A Appaloosas   **B** Sleipnir   **C** Palominos

Who is the legendary horse from Korean folklore?

A Chollima   **B** Chanwoo   **C** Cheolmin

CHAPTER 9

STAR-STUDDED STABLEMATES

Join us on a journey through time as we explore the lives of famous horses who left hoofprints on the annals of human history.

1.
Bucephalus was the beloved horse of Alexander the Great, known for his bravery and loyalty on the battlefield.

2.
Secretariat was a legendary racehorse, winning the Triple Crown in 1973 with record-breaking speed.

3.
Trigger was the famous horse of cowboy actor Roy Rogers, known for his intelligence and performing in many movies and shows.

4.
Comanche was a war horse who survived the Battle of the Little Bighorn.

5.
Copenhagen was the trusty steed of the Duke of Wellington, joining many battles during the Napoleonic Wars.

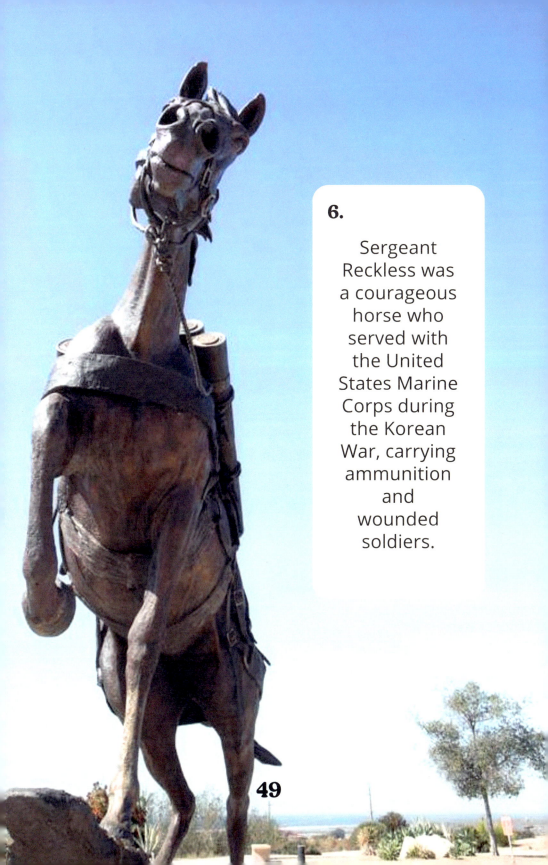

6.

Sergeant Reckless was a courageous horse who served with the United States Marine Corps during the Korean War, carrying ammunition and wounded soldiers.

7.

Blackie was a stunt horse in Hollywood, one of the most famous equine actors of his time.

8.

Marengo was the loyal horse of Napoleon Bonaparte, accompanying military campaigns across Europe.

9.

Snowman, also known as the "Cinderella Horse," was a plow horse turned champion show jumper,

10.

Muley was a workhorse during the construction of the Panama Canal.

TEST YOUR KNOWLEDGE!

Did you really absorb the new facts you have read about horses in this chapter?
Try answering the questions below:

Who was the loyal horse of Napoleon Bonaparte?

A Marengo   **B** Gerard   **C** Caroline

Who was the trusty steed of the Duke of Wellington?

A Copenhagen   **B** Cooper   **C** Clive

CHAPTER 10

RIDING INTO TOMORROW

Get ready to trot around the globe and discover the diverse roles horses play in the modern world, side by side with humans.

1.
Horses are cherished companions in countries worldwide, from the United States to Australia.

2.
Equine therapy programs help individuals with disabilities or mental health challenges globally.

3.
Horseback riding provides recreation and exercise in diverse landscapes, from Ireland to Argentina.

4.
Equestrian sports draw participants from countries such as France and the Netherlands.

5.
Horses assist with agriculture in countries like India and Brazil.

6.
Horse-drawn carriage tours are popular in cities like Vienna and New Orleans.

7.

Mounted police units patrol urban areas worldwide, including Paris and New York City.

8.

Guide horses aid visually impaired individuals in countries like the United States and Germany.

9.

The country Azerbaijan celebrates the Karabakh horse as its national animal.

10.

The USA has the most horses in any country in the world, possessing around 18% of the world's horses.

TEST YOUR KNOWLEDGE!

Did you really absorb the new facts you have read about horses in this chapter?
Try answering the questions below:

In India and Brazil, horses are known to help with this kind of work...

A Agriculture **B** Therapy **C** Law

This country celebrates a horse as its national animal...

A East Timor **B** Azerbaijan **C** Algeria

ANSWER KEY

Did you enjoy answering the questions at the end of each chapter? Here are the correct answers:

Chapter 1	Chapter 6
B,A	C,B
Chapter 2	Chapter 7
A,B	A,C
Chapter 3	Chapter 8
A,C	B,A
Chapter 3	Chapter 9
A,C	A,A
Chapter 3	Chapter 10
A,A	A,B

lemon cooks

Thank you for reading this fun fact book.

As the author, I hope you enjoyed learning through this book. To express my appreciation, please use the QR code below to access a free gift.

Get instant access to over 1,000 printable resources that you can use for learning in school or at home.

Made in United States
Cleveland, OH
22 April 2025

16351449R00036